THE POETRY PROCESSOR

BOOK 1

Paul Higgins

CONTENTS

TO THE STUDENT

The Poetry Processor gives you the chance to explore poetry, to write poems yourself, and to read and enjoy poems written by other people.

Poetry is powerful.
♦ Poetry can help you to use words more skilfully and imaginatively
♦ Poetry can help you to find pleasure in words
  – in their music, through rhythm, rhyme and sound
  – in their meanings, through wordplay and riddles
  – in their pattern, through the way they join together to make a whole poem
♦ Poetry can be a way of speaking about things that matter to you
♦ Poetry can make you more aware of the world around you
♦ Poetry can help you to discover things about yourself and other people
♦ Poetry can challenge, shock, provoke and surprise.

This book shows you some of the many different types of poetry that you can find, and that you can write anytime, anywhere.

Paul Higgins.

1 RHYME

What is rhyme? Divide into pairs and read aloud the poems below. Listen for the rhymes.

RHYMES   Spike Milligan

Eggs will rhyme with legs
But eggs aren't hairy or fat.
You can boil an egg for breakfast
But legs wouldn't stand for that!

Dog will rhyme with log
But a log isn't a man's best friend,
And you can't throw a dog on the fire,
If you did he'd be hard to mend.

Cat will rhyme with Hat,
But that my friend is all.
A Hat won't drink a bowl of milk
And you can't hang your cat in the hall!

Snake will rhyme with Lake
But only the Snake lays eggs.
Otherwise they are both identical,
For neither of them has legs!

Roses are red
Violets are blue
Some poems rhyme
This one doesn't.

Traditional

You can probably tell when one word rhymes with another. A rhyme is the end of one word sounding exactly the same as the end of another word. For example, in Spike Milligan's poem, hat rhymes with cat. Can you find any other words in the poem which rhyme with cat?

MORE THINGS TO DO

1. How many other words can you think of which rhyme with hat? Make a list. Here is the beginning of my list:

hat
mat
bat
fat

2. You can do this activity on your own, in pairs, or in small groups. Here is a list of words. Choose one of them and write down as many other words as you can think of which rhyme with the word you have chosen.

   IN   GO   LOG   FILL   IT   BAD   LOT   BED   HOOD   DOOR   DINE

I have picked DOOR. Here is the start of my list:

door
poor
your
or
score

The spelling does not have to be exactly the same, but the end sounds must match. If you are not sure whether one word rhymes with another, say them aloud, but quietly, to yourself and you should get a better idea. Do they rhyme?

3. You can turn activity 2 into a game called Rhyme Time.

   ♦ Get into pairs or small groups.
   ♦ Choose a word which you are all going to use.
   ♦ Set yourselves a limit of two minutes and each make a list of words which rhyme.
   ♦ The person who writes the list with the most rhyming words is the winner. Repeat the game and keep your score.

4. Rhymes aren't just used in poetry. Look for rhymes in adverts, jingles, birthday cards, posters, comics and magazines. Build up a collection. Bring your rhymes into an English lesson and read them out to the class. The whole class could make a wall display of the rhymes they have found. Leave spaces so that you can add a new rhyme from time to time.

2 RHYTHM

The world is full of rhythms. In pairs or small groups read aloud the writing below which is part of a poem.

> This...is...the...one...
> That...is...the...one...
> This is the one,
> That is the one,
> This is the one, that is the one
> This is the one, that is the one...
>
> Over the river, past the mill,
> Through the tunnel under the hill;
> Round the corner, past the wall,
> Through the wood where trees grow tall.
> Then in sight of the town by the river,
> Brake by the crossing where white leaves quiver.
> Slow as the streets of the town slide past
> And the windows stare
>   at the jerking of the coaches
>   Coming into the station approaches.
>
> Stop at the front.
> Stop at the front.
> Stop...at the front.
> Stop...at the...
> Stop.
>
> Ahhhh!

What does the rhythm in the poem remind you of? (The title of the poem is at the end of this unit.)

If you listen to a pop song, or any music, you will usually hear a rhythm. Your body has rhythms too. Your heartbeat and your breathing have rhythms, and both of these have a strong effect upon the rhythms of poetry and music.

A rhythm is a flow of beats or sounds.

6

MORE THINGS TO DO

1. Think of some more examples of rhythms. Make a list of them. Here is the beginning of my list:

heartbeats
breathing
the sound of a train
the sound of rain on a window-pane
a clock ticking
the sound of the sea
a washing machine
the banging of a hammer

2. Divide into pairs and practise reading aloud the poem at the beginning of the unit. How does the rhythm change as the poem goes on? Why does it change? Try to make your reading bring out the changes in the rhythm.

Types of Rhythms

There are many types of rhythms, but to make things easier we can divide them into two main types in poetry.

Type one: Where the rhythm is a regular flow of beats following a set pattern.

Type two: Where there is no set pattern and so the rhythm can change through the poem.

For now we are going to work on the first type, where the rhythm is a regular flow of beats.

RHYMES IN A RHYTHM

This is a simple game you can play to practise making rhymes in a rhythm. You can play it in pairs, small groups or as a whole class. If you are in a group:

◆ Arrange yourselves in a circle and choose a key rhyming word.
◆ Each player thinks of a word that rhymes with the key word.
◆ The group counts one, two, three – then, on the fourth beat, the first player says his/her chosen rhyming word.
◆ Continue this pattern for as many rounds as you wish.

If the word chosen was TIN, a round of the game might go like this:

1–2–3–

Player 1: WIN.

1–2–3–

Player 2: FIN.

1–2–3–

Player 3: GRIN.

1–2–3–

Player 4: IN. . . etc.

If you do not want to count you can clap quietly, but don't clap on the fourth beat – otherwise you won't hear the word being said.

You are out if you:

♦ don't say a word in time to the rhythm
♦ say a word which doesn't rhyme
♦ repeat a word that's already been said by someone else.

Here are some key rhyming words:
OIL   TO   ME   HIM   TIN   FAT   RED   WON   BET   SHOW   RIDE
HIT   FIGHT   GLAD   OUT   SING   AIR   DEAR   BEAT   I   ALL
STILL   SAY   USE   CAN   FAR   TIME   SHAM   HOT   COAL
GOOD   RUDE   CAP

When you have used one key word for a while, change it to another. If you get very good at the game you could reduce the number of beats between each word spoken, or perhaps make the rhythm faster.

The writing at the beginning of this unit is from 'The Song the Train Sang' by Neil Adams.

3 RHYME AND RHYTHM

In pairs or small groups, read the following two poems aloud, listening carefully to the rhythm of each poem.

CATS   Eleanor Farjeon

Cats sleep
Anywhere,
Any table,
Any chair,
Top of piano,
Window ledge,
In the middle,
On the edge,
Open drawer,
Empty shoe,
Anybody's
Lap will do,
Fitted in a
Cardboard box,
In the cupboard
With your frocks —
Anywhere!
They don't care!
Cats sleep
Anywhere.

UPSIDE DOWN   Aileen Fisher

It's funny how beetles
and creatures like that
can walk upside down
as well as walk flat:

They crawl on a ceiling
and climb on a wall
without any practice
or trouble at all,

While I have been trying
for a year (maybe more)
and still I can't stand
with my head on the floor.

The rhythm in poetry is normally made up of two types of beat: a light beat and a heavy beat or *stress*.

In both of the poems above there were two *stresses*, or heavy beats, to a line. We can mark the parts of the words where the stress falls with a dash, like this:

> Cāts slēep
> Ānywhēre,
> Āny tāble,
> Āny chāir...

> It's fūnny how bēetles
> and crēatures like thāt
> can wālk upside dōwn
> as wēll as walk flāt.

The poems both have two *stresses* to a line, but they have different rhythms. Can you say why?

The rhythms of the two poems are different because one poem has more *light* beats to a line than the other. If we mark a light beat with a curve like this˘, we can see which poem has more light beats to a line:

> Cats sleep
> Anўwhere,
> Anў tablĕ,
> Anў chair...

> Iť's funnў hŏw beetlĕs
> aňd creatŭres lĭke that
> căn walk uṗsĭde down
> aš well aš wălk flat.

Read the poems aloud again, this time listening for the light and heavy beats. Do you notice what happens to the rhythm when there are more light beats to a line?

Generally, the more light beats there are between the heavy ones, the faster the rhythm becomes. So the rhythms of the two poems are quite different, even though all the lines have two heavy beats or *stresses*.

If you put too many light beats in between the heavy ones, then you could lose the rhythm altogether. Normally, three light beats between every heavy one is the very most you should put in to make a clear rhythm, and it is usually better to stick to only one or two.

MORE THINGS TO DO

1. All the short lines below have two stresses in them. Read them aloud to each other to see if you can hear where the stresses are.

1. Joseph's log	11. Ginger pop	21. Eat a fig
2. All afloat	12. Too soon	22. Lumps of lead
3. Goose Fair	13. See you later	23. You're a twit
4. Brown Bess	14. I suppose	24. In the dirt
5. Bread and cheese	15. Jonah's whale	25. Pick up sticks
6. Brown Joe	16. Apples and pears	26. Over there
7. Cain and Abel	17. Mutton pies	27. Son and daughter
8. North and South	18. Plates of meat	28. Number three
9. East and West	19. Sugar and honey	29. Father and mother
10. Frog and toad	20. Have a fright	30. Sticks and stones

2. The lines have different numbers of light beats.

    a Can you find a line with no light beats?
    b Can you find a line with one light beat in between the two stresses?
    c Can you find a line with two light beats in between the two stresses?

3. Choose any of the short lines above and think of another line which rhymes with it and which has a two-stress rhythm. For example:

Āll aflōat
Īn a bōat

The lines don't have to make sense. For instance this would be just as good for the previous line:

All afloat
With a coat

What you must do is make sure that your end word rhymes, and that your line has two heavy beats. See how many you can do and how imaginative you can be. If you get really good at this you can write a whole group of lines with the same rhyme and two-stress rhythm:

All afloat
Like a stoat
In a boat
On a moat
With a coat
Round your throat.

When you have completed some examples, read them aloud to each other.

4 RHYMING SLANG

The lines below tell a simple story. Read it and see if you can tell what is happening.

HEARTS OF OAK   Paul Higgins

The currant bun was shining
So I went for a ball and chalk.
I met a china plate of mine.
We started to rabbit and pork.

He told me a Daily Mail.
He was in a two-and-eight.
Could he have some bees and honey
From his very best china plate?

Now he wasn't a holy friar.
I could tell this wasn't a joke.
So I gave him some of my sausage and mash
Because he was hearts of oak.

He put it in his Lucy Locket.
He said he'd pay back what he owed
And with a smile all over his boat race
He went off down the frog and toad.

The lines are written using a rhyming slang which was developed in the East End of London – originally, it is said, as a secret language to outwit the police.

Find out exactly what is happening in the poem above by reading the list of rhyming slang terms below and then reading the poem aloud in ordinary English. (The title is in rhyming slang, too.)

currant bun – sun   ball and chalk – walk
china plate – mate   rabbit and pork – talk
Daily Mail – tale   two-and-eight – state
bees and honey – money   (in a state – upset)
sausage and mash – cash   holy friar – liar
hearts of oak – broke   Lucy Locket – pocket
boat race – face   frog and toad – road

MORE THINGS TO DO

Below is a short dictionary of more rhyming slang terms. To get used to using rhyming slang, write *A Day in the Life of a Cockney*, using rhyming slang where you can. You can use the expressions in the list plus any others that you may know. Here is the start of my *Day in the Life of a Cockney*.

> *I woke up and rubbed my mince pies. I got up and went to the bathroom for a bubble and squash. I brushed my Hampstead Heath and combed my Barnet Fair. I went down the apples and pears and made myself a cup of Rosy Lea . . . . .*

bank – iron tank
phone – dog and bone
beer – pig's ear
boots – daisy roots
bread – Uncle Fred
brother – one 'n' t'other
butter – stammer and stutter
car – jam jar
clock – dickory dock
deaf – Mutt and Jeff
dinner – Jim Skinner
  – Lilley and Skinner
drunk – elephant's trunk
eyes – mince pies
fag – Harry Rag
  – oily rag
feet – plates of meat
flowers – April showers
  – early hours
Flying Squad (Police) – Sweeney Todd
hair – Barnet Fair
hands – German bands
hat – tit for tat

head – crust of bread
hot – peas in the pot
house – cat and mouse
kids – dustbin lids
  – saucepan lids
luck – Donald Duck
lunch – kidney punch
mince pies – eyes
mouth – north and south
nose – I suppose
old man (husband) – pot and pan
park – Noah's Ark
phone – dog and bone
pig – addley dig
pinch – half inch
pocket – sky rocket
pub – rub-a-dub
shave – dig in the grave
shirt – Dicky Dirt
shovel – Lord Lovell
sick – Moby Dick
sister – skin and blister
sleep – Bo Peep
smoke – laugh 'n' joke

soap – Cape of Good Hope
socks – China rocks
  – almond rocks
stairs – apples and pears
stink – pen and ink
suit – white and flute
table – Cain and Abel
talk – rabbit and pork
tea – Rosy Lea
teeth – Hampstead Heath
telly – custard and jelly
thief – tea leaf
ticket – bat and wicket
time – Harry Lime
  – bird lime
trousers – round the houses
wash – bubble and squash
water – fisherman's daughter
wife – trouble and strife
word – dicky bird

Tap The Beat
With Your Plates of Meat

When you use rhyming slang, you replace the ordinary word with an expression that rhymes with it. But you may have noticed that, not only does cockney slang rhyme, all the terms have a two-stress rhythm also:

trousers – rōund the hōuses
nose – Ī suppōse
kids – dūstbin līds

The terms have a rhythm. They all have two heavy beats.

MORE THINGS TO DO

1. Make up an entirely new slang of your own following the same two-stress rhythm. You could start by making up new terms for some of the words in the list above: for example for 'stink' instead of 'pen and ink' you could have 'down the sink'.

   Then you could use words not in the list: snow, card, tree, shop, fire, chair, bowl, soup or any other words you want.

   > REMEMBER
   > ♦ Your slang must rhyme
   > ♦ Your rhyming slang words need a two-stress rhythm

2. When you have become experts in rhyming slang, divide into pairs and write a conversation or a short play in rhyming slang and then read it aloud, or even perform it. You could even try to rabbit and pork using the slang terms where you can. Try it and see if you can keep a conversation going for two cock linnets.

5 COUPLETS

A couplet is two lines of poetry which go together. The pairs of lines are called couplets because they are in *couples*. Read the two poems below which use couplets.

TWO SAD William Cole

It's such a shock, I almost screech
When I find a worm inside my peach!
But then what really makes me blue
Is to find a worm who's bit in two!

COUSIN JANE Colin West

Yesterday my cousin Jane
Said she was an aeroplane
But I wanted further proof
So I pushed her off the roof.

How many couplets are there in each poem above?

The two lines of a couplet do not always have to rhyme, but in this unit we will work with rhyming couplets.

Single Couplets

A poem can be made up of many couplets, but a single couplet can also be a poem on its own, like these examples.

LULLABY Adrian Henri

Imagine being asleep in the deep
Counting whales instead of sheep.

BEES   Russell Hoban

Honey bees are very tricky —
Honey doesn't make them sticky.

DEAR SIR   Anon

Sir is kind and sir is gentle
Sir is strong and sir is mental.

P'S AND Q'S   Roger McGough

I puite often confuse
My quecs and poos.

THE CITY   Daniel Wischhusen

People rushing everywhere
Is there nobody to care?

THE PARENT   Ogden Nash

Children aren't happy with nothing to ignore,
And that's what parents were created for.

THE DESIRED SWAN-SONG   Samuel Taylor Coleridge

Swans sing before they die — 'twere no bad thing
Should certain persons die before they sing.

In pairs or small groups, read through the single couplet poems again. Even though the poems are short, they all have ideas in them. In your groups, talk about the ideas that you get from the poems.

MORE THINGS TO DO

1. Below is a list of single words. Imagine that each word is the first rhyming word of a couplet. To get practice in writing couplets, pick one or two examples and complete the two lines.

To do this you will need to

♦ find a rhyme for the second line
♦ use a regular rhythm.

For example, ... bus
....

could be completed like this:

I never catch a bus
The waiting's too much fuss.

or like this:

A double decker bus
Is simply ludicrous.

.... car   .... flower
....

.... hill   .... time
....

.... stream   .... tent
....

.... school   .... sing
....

.... jam   .... frog
....

.... tree   .... sky
....

2. Now try writing some one-couplet poems yourself from scratch. They can
   be about anything you like. It is a good idea to write the couplets in rough
   first, either on note paper or in the back of your exercise book, because you
   will probably make changes as you write them. When you have written a
   couplet that you are happy with, copy it out neatly into the front of your
   book. You could draw pictures to go with your couplets.

REMEMBER
♦ You need two lines.
♦ The lines should rhyme.
♦ Each line begins with a capital letter.
♦ You should use a regular rhythm (the same number of STRESSES
  in each line).

When you have finished writing your couplets, you could get into groups and
read them to one another or make a wall display of your couplets with
illustrations.

6 MORE COUPLETS

A couplet can be a poem on its own (see Unit 5), but usually it is part of a longer poem which is built up from a number of couplets. In pairs, read the poems below and discuss the question which follows each one.

ANCIENT HISTORY   Arthur Guiterman

I hope the old Romans
Had painful abdomens.

I hope that the Greeks
Had toothache for weeks.

I hope the Egyptians
Had chronic conniptions.

I hope that the Arabs
Were bitten by scarabs.

I hope that the Vandals
Had thorns in their sandals.

I hope that the Persians
Had gout in all versions.

I hope that the Medes
Were kicked by their steeds.

They started the fuss
And left it to us!

How does the writer feel about 'Ancient History'? (If you don't know the meaning of some of the words, look them up in a dictionary.)

BAT   Theodore Roethke

By day the bat is cousin to the mouse.
He likes the attic of an ageing house.

His fingers make a hat about his head.
His pulse beat is so slow we think him dead.

He loops in crazy figures half the night
Among the trees that face the corner light.

But when he brushes up against a screen,
We are afraid of what our eyes have seen:

For something is amiss or out of place
When mice with wings can wear a human face.

How does the writer think we feel about the bat?

This next poem is about a certain English teacher. The couple who wrote it used couplets. There is a picture to go with it. The poem finishes on page 20.

MR. HIGGINS   Tony Becker and Daniel Wischhusen

There's no-one like our English teacher,
He acts just like he's a preacher.

He's got a fuzz ball on his head
And his ears go beetroot red.

He wears a knitted sock for a tie,
He is a nit and that's why.

We've got a teacher who thinks he's hard,
He's about as hard as a bit of card.

All he ever does is nag
He's as useful as a stubbed-out fag.

He likes to lie about his age
He reckons flares are all the rage.

PARIS '86

His shoes are so old-fogeyish
I bet they smell of tuna fish.

He carries a tatty, black brief-case
And leaves it all around the place.

He likes to think he can play the guitar
In his mind he's a megastar.

He prefers to wear soft contact lenses
He buys them on the cheap from Menzies.

We know that his first name is Paul
It should be Lanky, he's so tall.

He's got the worst car in the school
It's slower than a clapped-out mule.

He always looks like he's slept rough,
That's why he thinks he's tough.

How do the writers feel about their English teacher?

MORE THINGS TO DO

Write a poem in couplets about either
a an animal, or
b a person

You could choose your English teacher, but that might be risky!

- In rough, write down the things which come into your mind in connection with the subject of your poem.
- Then ask yourself
  a which details are important and should go in your poem
  b how you *feel* about the animal or person you are writing about.
- Then begin to write a first version of your poem in the back of your book or on rough paper. You will probably make lots of changes as you are writing. When you have finished your poem and you are happy with it, write it out neatly in your English book. You could draw a picture to go with it too.

7 DOWN BEHIND THE DUSTBIN

Here is a poem by Michael Rosen.

DOWN BEHIND THE DUSTBIN

Down behind the dustbin
I met a dog called Ted.
'Leave me alone,' he says,
'I'm just going to bed.'

Down behind the dustbin
I met a dog called Felicity.
'It's a bit dark here,' she said,
'They've cut off the electricity.'

Down behind the dustbin
I met a dog called Roger.
'Do you own this bin?' I said.
'No. I'm only the lodger.'

Down behind the dustbin
I met a dog called Sue.
'What are you doing here?' I said.
'I've got nothing else to do.'

Down behind the dustbin
I met a dog called Anne.
'I'm just off now,' she said,
'to see a dog about a man.'

Down behind the dustbin
I met a dog called Jack.
'Are you going anywhere?' I said.
'No. I'm just coming back.'

Down behind the dustbin
I met a dog called Billy.
'I'm not talking to you,' I said,
'if you're going to be silly.'

Down behind the dustbin
I met a dog called Barry.
He tried to take the bin away
but it was too heavy to carry.

Down behind the dustbin
I met a dog called Mary.
'I wish I wasn't a dog,' she said,
'I wish I was a canary.'

This is a poem which is organised into regular groups of lines, or *stanzas*. A stanza can be very short, with just a few lines, as in this poem, or it can be very long, with many lines. A stanza is a section of a poem.

How many stanzas are there in the poem above? How many lines are there in each stanza?

Discuss or write answers to the following questions:

a What is the first line of each stanza?
b What is the second line of each stanza?
c What changes in the second line from stanza to stanza?
d Which lines rhyme?
e How many stresses (heavy beats) are there in each line? (Be careful. One line has one stress more than the rest.)

MORE THINGS TO DO

If you have answered the questions above you should have a good idea of how the poem works. Now write a 'Down Behind the Dustbin' poem yourself.

Down behind the dustbin
I met a dog called ...

8 FREE-VERSE POEMS

So far the poems you have been writing have had regular rhythm and rhyme schemes. But poems do not *have* to rhyme or have a regular rhythm. Read the poem below. It was written by a twelve-year-old girl.

AN INJECTION   Janet Clark

We stampede down the corridor,
Each holding a white card.
Fingering it like some poisonous insect.
Will it hurt?
The thud of our feet echoes our drumming hearts.
'Bags last!'
'I'm going last.'
'I'm not going first.'
'Me neither.'
We stand in line,
Like prisoners waiting for execution.
I'm not scared.
I try to sound heroic.
I drift. . .
Into a senseless dream.
I snap out of it as my friend jolts me,
Saying, 'Go on, it's you next.'
I march stiffly towards the door.
The nurse motions me to the chair.
The saliva refuses to enter my mouth.
The blue-flamed bunsen burner hisses slightly.
The drab, grey walls seem more depressing than usual.
My sleeve is pushed roughly up.
The strong stench of disinfectant bites my nostrils.
My arm is touched with something cold.
I shudder violently.
It brushes my arm
Soothingly.
Everyone falls silent.
It's over!
A mere pin prick.
A bubble of blood
Dribbles down my arm.
It's absorbed by a piece of lint.
A gush of breath rushes out.
The air seems clearer.
My mind fresher.
'Next please.'

23

Discuss the following questions in pairs or small groups. Make brief notes of your answers.

a What things do you notice about the way the poem is set out?
b How long are the lines?
c Does the poem have a regular rhythm?
d Does it have a rhythm at all?
e Which words or phrases do you find interesting or enjoyable? Explain why.

Writing Free-Verse

'An Injection' is a free-verse poem. This means that there is no regular rhythm or rhyme scheme. This is a fine poem because the writer has thought carefully about the words she has used and the way she has arranged them.

Although the writer has not used a regular rhyme scheme, some sounds in the poem do rhyme to give a particular effect.

> 'A gush of breath rushes out'

What is the effect of the rhyming 'ush' sounds here?

Although she has not used a regular rhythm, the writer has varied the length of the lines very carefully and deliberately, and not just at random.

Some lines are very short and sharp, creating a jerky rhythm:

> 'Bags last!'
> 'I'm going last.'
> 'I'm not going first.'

Some are long, creating the effect of stillness:

> 'The blue-flamed bunsen burner hisses slightly.'

Why does the writer create this jerky rhythm?
Why does she create a feeling of stillness in the rhythm?

MORE THINGS TO DO

Pick an experience that you have had which at the time was painful or scary, troubling, worrying, upsetting or nerve-wracking, and write a free-verse poem about it. But before you do this, read the next section.

Drafting

Don't just write your poem without preparation. Do it by preparing a *draft* of the poem. A *draft* spelt like this is not something which blows under your door (a draught); it is the first version or rough copy of a piece of writing.

You can make a draft of your poem in clear stages.

♦ First of all write down the main idea for the poem in just a few words, for example, 'When I broke my leg'.
♦ Next, quickly write down, in any order, all the words, thoughts and feelings that come into your mind that are connected with the experience. In other words, brainstorm it. (You do not have to use sentences at this stage.)
♦ When you have completed the brainstorming, read your words and phrases, underlining the interesting ones which you will want to put directly into your poem. Then, if necessary, sort them into an order.
♦ Now write the first draft of your poem.

To show you in more detail exactly how this is done, here are the stages of my draft of a poem about an incident which happened to me:

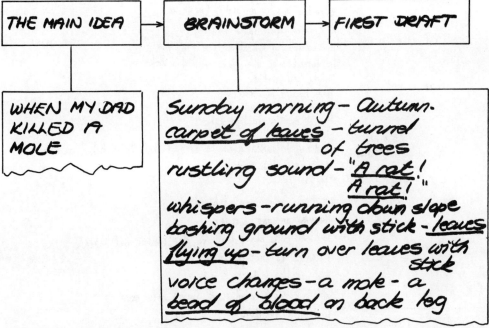

On pages 26 and 27 are my first draft and my final copy of the poem. You will see the corrections and changes I made as I was writing and all the decisions I had to make before I got to the final version. Compare the two versions. Did I make the right decisions?

My dad and I

Enjoying a the quiet of a Sunday morning

Walked through a long tunnel of trees

Which was as dark as an underground cavern

Leaves lay on the ground like a soft, damp carpet

He held the hefty switch

Which he had cut from a tree.

He said a big stick made him feel safer.

Suddenly he stopped froze

His arms stretched out ↑

(His head twisted to one side)

I heard his a whisper

~~As if from a stranger's voice~~

"A rat! A rat!."

Then he tore off

Down the slope

In an explosion of energy (?)

I saw him in the distance

Beating the side of the hill

~~Madly insanely~~ With mad ferocious strokes

Brown leaves flew up ↑

(In a startled shower)

I reached him

Uncertain and // afraid   (new line)

He panted and spoke eagerly:

"It's-a rat! I - think I've - got him!"

He turned over the leaves with his stick

Slowly and gently

Then I heard his voice again

But it had changed.

He let out a cracked sigh.

"It's a mole."

(through the shade) And // I looked down on the spot that the stick had uncovered

And there lay a mole

Dead

Just a single bead of blood

Beaming on one back leg

To show the blows that the tiny creature had taken.

I wanted to pick it up

And cradle it back to life

But we covered it with leaves once more

And left it there.

We walked on

Though in my heart

I wanted to go back home.

A MOMENT'S BLINDNESS   Paul Higgins

My dad and I
Enjoying the quiet of a Sunday morning
Walked through a long tunnel of trees
Which was as dark as an underground cavern.
Leaves lay on the ground like a soft, damp carpet.
He gripped the hefty switch
Which he had cut from a tree.
He said a big stick made him feel safer.
It was the instinct of the hunter, he said.
Suddenly he froze
His arms stretched out, his head twisted to one side.
I heard a hoarse whisper:
'A rat! A rat!'
Then he tore off
Down the slope
In a blind rush.
I saw him in the distance
Beating the side of the hill
With mad, ferocious strokes.
Brown leaves flew up in a startled shower.
I reached him
Afraid
Uncertain.
He panted and spoke eagerly:
'It's — a rat! I — think I've — got him!'
He turned over the leaves with his stick
Slowly and gently.
Then I heard his voice again
But it had changed.
He let out a cracked sigh.
'It's a mole.'
And through the gloom
My eyes fixed on the spot that the stick had uncovered
And there lay a mole
Dead
Just a single bead of blood, deep red
Beaming on one back leg
To show the blows that the tiny creature had taken.
I wanted to pick it up
And cradle it back to life
But we covered it with leaves
And left it there.
We walked on to the light
But in my mind
All I could see
Was a small blind face in the leaves.

As you can see, in the first version my poem didn't have a title. Thinking of a title is often the point when you find out what you are really trying to say in a poem. When I started to write, I wasn't intending to write about blindness, so why do you think I ended up calling the poem 'A Moment's Blindness'? How has this affected the way the poem has turned out?

Symbols

When you are writing a draft you can use symbols as shorthand for the corrections you want to make. Here are the symbols I used in my draft and what they mean:

mostly = words crossed out

// = new line

( )⟶↑ = move the words in brackets to where the arrow is pointing

λ = put the words at the top of the symbol in between the words either side of it

⤺⤻ = swap the words around

(?) = words could be changed/improved

You don't have to use symbols. If you do, you don't have to use the ones I used. You could make up a few of your own. But if you do use symbols, don't have too many, keep them simple, and use them in the same way throughout the draft.

Once you have written a draft of your poem, work on it to turn it into a final copy.

REMEMBER
♦ Your poem should not have a regular rhythm (but the length of the lines is still important).
♦ Your poem should not have a regular rhyme scheme (but some words can rhyme here and there if you want them to).
♦ Each line should begin with a capital letter.
♦ The choice of words is very important if your poem is to work well.

---

9 SPEAKING VOICES

Poetry isn't just about reading and writing words on a page. It's about speaking, hearing and feeling them too.

The poem below is best spoken and heard. Divide into pairs or small groups. Share the reading of this poem aloud, taking it in turns to speak a few lines each.

THE COMMENTATOR   Gareth Owen

Good afternoon and welcome
To this international
Between England and Holland
Which is being played here today
At 4, Florence Terrace.
And the pitch looks in superb condition
As Danny Markey, the England captain,
Puts England on the attack.
Straight away it's Markey
With a lovely little pass to Keegan,
Keegan back to Markey,
Markey in possession here
Jinking skilfully past the dustbins;
And a neat flick inside the cat there.
What a brilliant player this Markey is
And he's still only nine years old!
Markey to Francis,
Francis back to Markey,
Markey is through, he's through,
No, he's been tackled by the drainpipe;
But he's won the ball back brilliantly
And he's advancing on the Dutch keeper,
It must be a goal.
The keeper's off his line
But Markey chips him superbly
And it's a goal
No!
It's gone into Mrs Spence's next door.
And Markey's going round to ask for his ball back,
It could be the end of this international.
Now the door's opening
And yes, it's Mrs Spence,
Mrs Spence has come to the door.

Wait a minute
She's shaking her head, she is shaking her head,
She's not going to let England have their ball back.
What is the referee going to do?
Markey's coming back looking very dejected,
And he seems to be waiting. . .
He's going back,
Markey is going back for that ball!
What a brilliant and exciting move!
He waited until the front door was closed
And then went back for that ball.
And wait a minute,
He's found it, Markey has found that ball,
He has found that ball
And that's wonderful news
For the hundred thousand fans gathered here
Who are showing their appreciation
In no uncertain fashion.
But wait a minute,
The door's opening once more.
It's her, Mrs Spence
And she's waving her fist
And shouting something I can't quite understand
But I don't think it's encouragement.
And Markey's off,
He's jinked past her on the outside
Dodging this way and that
With Mrs Spence in hot pursuit.
And he's past her, he's through,
What skills this boy has!
But Mr Spence is there too,
Mr Spence in the sweeper role
With Rover their dog.
Markey's going to have to pull out all the stops now.
He's running straight at him,
And he's down, he's down on all fours!
What is he doing?
And Oh my goodness that was brilliant,
That was absolutely brilliant,
He's dived through Spence's legs;
But he's got him,
This rugged stopper has him by the coat
And Rover's barking in there too;
He'll never get out of this one.
But this is unbelievable!

He's got away
He has got away:
He wriggled out of his coat
And left part of his trousers with Rover.
This boy is real dynamite.
He's over the wall
He's clear
They'll never catch him now.
He's down the yard and on his way
And I don't think we're going to see
Any more of Markey
Until it's safe to come home.

Imagining a commentary on things that you are doing is something many people do at one time or another. In commentaries, though we might not normally notice it, words are spoken in a particular way.

Read Gareth Owen's poem again. What do you notice about the way words are being spoken? What impression does the commentary give you of what is happening?

Here is a 'commentator' poem by a pupil.

THE COMMENTATOR   Marc Sinfield

And he is off on this marathon of a journey,
One of the toughest races of his life so far,
This dangerous task at two-thirty a.m. to pinch, yes pinch
The Golden Delicious out of the fridge.
And already a quarter of the way there,
He is out of the bedroom,
And he said he would go for a world record time
Set by the next door neighbour Alan Jones.
And the time at his first lap marker is . . . 19.5 seconds!
Incredible! 0.62 seconds inside the world record.
My word, he is in tremendous form.
But there could be trouble.
He can feel his mum breathing down his neck.
And fortunately for him it's the wind from the bedroom,
But he has slowed considerably.
His second lap marker is 28.6 seconds
And that is an average time as he approaches the stairs.
And he grits his teeth as he tiptoes quickly down the stairs.
My goodness, he is a gutsy character.
He certainly needs to be now because he has reached the
    breaking point
Hit or bust.

Can he get past this Doberman without waking him?
These are tense moments and . . .
The dog has an eyelid open.
This is it, surely.
He cannot escape this catastrophe!
But wait!
Can he? Will he? Has he?
HE HAS!
My word what skill.
He stopped stone dead and the dog never saw him
So he can now carry on.
He is unstoppable as he oozes round the kitchen door
And whips open the fridge.
And he has won the Golden Delicious
And in a time which has lopped 0.46 seconds off the world
   record!
WHAT A PERFORMANCE!
But wait! This is nasty. Is it foot−?
Yes, it is footsteps.
Oh no, it's Mother.
And this is surely disqualification.
What a tragedy!
He must be heartbroken.
And his mum doesn't look too pleased
From the way she clouted him round the earhole.
What a shame that such an incredible feat
Has been marred by disqualification for being too noisy.
Well, that's it from Cheshunt tonight
So back to the studio!

On your own or in groups, choose one of the two 'commentator' poems above and practise reading it aloud for a performance to the rest of the class. Try to make it sound as close to an actual commentary as you can. You could also make a tape recording of your reading.

MORE THINGS TO DO

1. Write a 'commentator' poem of your own. Take a simple event, action or job and give a sports commentary that makes it sound as if it's the most exciting thing in the world.

   You will need to decide which type of sports commentary you are going to use. It could be tennis, horse-racing, snooker, football etc.

   This is a free-verse poem, so it doesn't rhyme. What is important is to try to capture the rhythms, the repetitions, the expressions – the *flow* of the way of speaking you hear in a sports commentary.

2. So far you have been working on a commentator's way of speaking, but there are many other examples of people speaking in a particular way according to the type of job they do. Here is a list of some of them:

   ◆ a teacher in front of a class
   ◆ a priest giving a sermon
   ◆ a policeman giving a crime report
   ◆ a headteacher giving an assembly
   ◆ a newsreader
   ◆ a disc jockey
   ◆ a lawyer in court
   ◆ a politician making a speech
   ◆ a sergeant major shouting instructions

   You can add more examples to the list.

   You could write another 'speaking voice' poem describing a simple action or event using the style of one of the people on the list.

   ◆ Think about how your chosen person talks.
   ◆ Write down a few common phrases they might use.
   ◆ Think of a simple action to describe.
   ◆ Then begin your poem.

   When you have completed it, read it out to a partner or to the class. You could also make a tape recording of it.

10 LISTS

A list poem is a list which is held together with an idea and a poetic shape, such as a rhyme pattern and a regular rhythm.

Here are some poems based on lists of objects and people.

Objects

Many of you may be able to remember some objects from the traditional list song 'The Twelve Days of Christmas'. Here is the list from the twelfth day downwards to remind you:

Twelve lords a-leaping, eleven ladies dancing, ten pipers piping, nine drummers drumming, eight maids a-milking, seven swans a-swimming, six geese a-laying, five gold rings, four calling birds, three French hens, two turtle doves and a partridge in a pear tree.

The following two poems contain lists of objects. The first one also uses the idea of a Christmas present list.

MY CHRISTMAS LIST   Gyles Brandreth

A police car
A helicopter
A gun that goes pop
A Frisbee
A ball
An Action Man that won't stop
A torch
A guitar
A printing set with ink
A bouncer
A new bear
A submarine that won't sink
A sword
A typewriter
A stove so I can cook
A radio
A Wendy house
Another dinosaur book –
Of course, Father Christmas, it's clearly understood
That I'll only get all of this if I'm specially good.

What would your Christmas list include?

the electric household Wes Magee

cooker   blanket
  toothbrush   fire
iron   light bulb
  tv   dryer
'fridge   radio
  robot   drill
toaster   speaker
  kettle   grill
slicer   grinder
  meters   fan
slide projector
  deep   fry pan
vacuum cleaner
  fuses   shocks
freezer   shaver
  junction box
water heater
  time switch   lamps
knife   recorder
  cables   amps
door chimes   organ
  infra red
guitar   video
  sunlamp bed
heated   rollers
  current   watts
train   adaptor
  bulkhead   spots
synthesizer
  night light glow
calculator
  stereo
cultivator
  metronome
volts   hair crimper
  ohm sweet ohm

♦ What idea ties this list together? (What do all these items have in common?)
♦ Is there a regular rhyme and rhythm?

People

These two poems are based on lists of people. The first one is set in a situation which should be familiar.

MORNING BREAK   Wes Magee

Andrew Flag plays football
Jane swings from the bars
Chucker Peach climbs drainpipes
Spike is seeing stars

Little Paul's a Martian
Anne walks on her toes
Ian Dump fights Kenny
Russell picks his nose

Dopey Di does hop-scotch
Curly drives a train
Maddox-Brown and Thompson
Stuff shoes down the drain

Lisa Thin throws netballs
Mitchell stands and stares
Nuttall from the first year
Shouts and spits and swears

Dick Fish fires his ray gun
Gaz has stamps to swop
Dave and Dan are robbers
Teacher is the cop

Betty Blob pulls faces
Basher falls and dies
Tracey shows her knickers
Loony swallows flies

Faye sits in a puddle
Trev is eating mud
Skinhead has a nosebleed
– pints and pints of blood

Robbo Lump pings marbles
Murray hands out cake
What a lot of nonsense
During
   Morning
     Break

BEST FRIENDS   Adrian Henri

It's Susan I talk to not Tracey,
Before that I sat next to Jane;
I used to be best friends with Lynda
But these days I think she's a pain.

Natasha's all right in small doses,
I meet Mandy sometimes in town;
I'm jealous of Annabel's pony
And I don't like Nicola's frown.

I used to go skating with Catherine,
Before that I went there with Ruth;
And Kate's so much better at trampoline:
She's a showoff, to tell you the truth.

I think that I'm going off Susan,
She borrowed my comb yesterday;
I think I might sit next to Tracey,
She's my nearly best friend: she's O.K.

Why is this poem called 'Best Friends'?

MORE THINGS TO DO

Write a list poem of either (a) objects, or (b) people.

Here is a list of topics you can write about:

crazes	television	transport	food
Easter	animals	relations	school
a disco	teachers	a wedding	friends

Or you can write about any subject that you are interested in, or which you know a lot about.

Writing a List Poem
♦ Choose a subject which interests you, such as Pollution.
♦ Make a list of objects or people connected with the subject.
♦ Read the list carefully and decide what you are going to make your list say. What idea will hold it together?
♦ Rewrite it putting the details into the order which you think is best. You can add a rhyme and rhythm pattern if you wish.

My List

To show you in more detail how to do this, here is how I used my chosen topic of Pollution.

Here is my list.

DDT
Car exhaust fumes
nuclear waste
acid rain
radiation
oil
dead fish
toxic chemicals
stinking sewage

I looked at my list and decided that the idea of progress would tie the list together. I wanted to show that progress can be destructive. I then decided to use a regular rhyme and rhythm. This is my finished list poem:

IN THE GREENHOUSE   Paul Higgins

Car exhaust fumes
Oil in the sea
Smoke from factories
DDT
Radiation
Nuclear waste
Toxic chemicals
Toxic taste
Power stations
Acid rain
Poisons in the
Food Chain
CO2
Greenhouse gas
Down the river
Dead fish pass

Stinking sewage
Withered trees
Ozone layer
CFCs
The clearest water
Of a lifeless lake
All these things done
For our sake
Seals wiped out
To our shame
All these things done
In the name
of Progress

Now choose your topic and write your list poem.

11 ALPHABET POEMS

It is important to learn the alphabet not only to read, but also because it is the order in which many kinds of information are arranged, such as words in a dictionary, names in a telephone directory, or indexes of street names. Can you think of any other information which is arranged in alphabetical order?

The alphabet can be a way of organising a poem, too.

THE ALPHABET OF MY DISLIKES   Clare Wallace

A is for ants which attack your pants, admiring almost any material.
B is for brothers who bully and boss always bragging because they
  are bigger.
C is for camp and all that cooking, eating crusty currant cake with
  stodgy custard.
D is for demons, devilishly devouring detestable doted on
  children.
E is for ecstatic relatives enjoying embarrassing each one of the
  family.
F is for famine, forbidding and far off, famishing other people.
G is for gardens, groaning, grunting and grumbling when they get
  desperate for weeding.
H is for hurricanes, hurling and whirling hurrying by.
I is for idiots who are idle and impudent and very ignorant.
J is for junk joining other jumbled jumble.
K is for ketchup, King of the kitchen sauces and he knows it too.
L is for lions, the lordly beasts looking down on lower animals.
M is for maths making a miserable person of me and many of
  mankind.
N is for nasty newts hiding behind nine rocks.
O is for octopus, King of the ocean of small fish.
P is for pests persisting in perpetually talking to you.
Q is for quills making questions and answers.
R is for ratty people rabbitting roughly on for some unreasonable
  reason.
S is for snakes, sliding and slithering, slyly swallowing some
  unsuspecting subject.
T is for tarantula with a big temper, very touchy, temperamental and
  furry.
U is for umbrellas, urgently urging their way towards me when it's
  sunny.
V is for vanity, very frustrating and very annoying.

W is for wallies that wear white wellies and wide-brimmed wicker
   washing baskets on their heads when it's foggy!
X is for X-rays where x-cellent doctors get x-cited because
   of the x-hilarating operation.
Y is for yaks which yak and yak and yak and then start yawning.
Z is for zombies with zero zest and absolutely no zoom.

This writer has used the alphabet to make a poem, but she hasn't just set
out each item in alphabetical order. Look again at the poem. What else
has she done with each letter in turn?

> B is for brothers who bully and boss always bragging because
>   they are bigger.

She has repeated the particular sound of each letter as many times in the
line as she can. In the example above she has repeated the sound of 'B'.

She has repeated the vowels, which are a, e, i, o, u and sometimes y:

> A is for ants which attack your pants, admiring almost any
>   material.

How many times does she repeat the 'A' here?
How many times does she repeat the 'I' in that line?

She has repeated the consonants, which are all the other letters:

> S is for snakes, sliding and slithering, slyly swallowing some
>   unsuspecting subject.

How many times has she repeated the 'S' sound here?
How many times has she repeated 'T' in that line?

There are special names for repeating consonant sounds
and vowel sounds in poetry.

Repeating the same consonant sound gives a sound effect
in poetry which is called ALLITERATION.

Repeating the same vowel sound gives a sound effect
which is called ASSONANCE.

Read the poem carefully again and pick two more lines which use alliteration and two which use assonance. Compare your choices with the lines chosen by a partner.

MORE THINGS TO DO

1. Pick a consonant or a vowel. Now make up one or two sentences in which you repeat that letter as often as you can. Then decide whether you have used assonance or alliteration. Here is an example:

Mitch the magical monkey made marvellous moves in mid-air, but he managed to miss a massive branch and so he plummeted to the amazing, marshy mounds below. Miraculously and magnificently he remained unharmed, though mildly messy.

2. Now you can try to write your own alphabet poem, but you may find writing a whole alphabet poem yourself too much to do, so you could work with others in pairs, small groups or as a whole class, with each person taking a different letter or letters.

   ◆ Pick a subject such as Likes, Dislikes, Food, Animals, the place where you live or anything you know a lot about.
   ◆ If you're working in groups, decide who is going to tackle which letters.
   ◆ Begin working on the letters. If you get stuck on one letter then leave it and go on to another one and come back to it later.
   ◆ Start each line with 'A is for. . ./B is for . . . etc.'
   ◆ Repeat the consonant sound or vowel sound as many times as you can in the same line.
   ◆ Put all the lines together to make the finished alphabet poem. If you decide to write a class poem, when it is finished you could go round the class, each person reading out a line or lines of the poem.

REMEMBER
◆ Each line starts 'A is for. . ./ B is for . . . etc.'
◆ You repeat the first letter of the line as many times as you can in the same line.

---

12 TONGUE TWISTERS

In pairs, try to read these four lines aloud without getting your tongue in a twist.

> A twister of twists once twisted a twist,
> The twist that he twisted was a three-twisted twist;
> If in twisting the twist, one twist should untwist,
> The untwisted twist would untwist the twist.

In tongue twisters the same sounds are often repeated. Which sound in the name 'tongue twisters' is used three times? Which sound is used twice? Here is another familiar tongue twister:

> Peter Piper picked a peck of pickled pepper;
> Did Peter Piper pick a peck of pickled pepper?
> If Peter Piper picked a peck of pickled pepper,
> Where's the peck of pickled pepper Peter Piper picked?

Obviously the p is re-pea-ted here, but what other consonants are repeated, too?

Tongue twisters often use alliteration (repeated consonant sounds) and assonance (repeated vowel sounds).

Here are some more examples of tongue twisters. Get into pairs or small groups and practise reading them aloud and see how fast you can read them without making any mistakes.

> Careful Katie cooked a crisp and crinkly cabbage;
> Did careful Katie cook a crisp and crinkly cabbage?
> If careful Katie cooked a crisp and crinkly cabbage,
> Where's the crisp and crinkly cabbage careful Katie cooked?

She sells seashells on the seashore;
The shells that she sells are seashells I'm sure.
So if she sells seashells on the sea shore,
I'm sure that the shells are seashore shells.

Red lorry, yellow lorry.

Swan swam over the sea,
Swim swan swim.
Swan swam back again;
Well swum swan.

BETTY BOTTER
Betty Botter bought some butter,
But she said, 'This butter's bitter.
If I put it in my batter
It will make my batter bitter.
But a bit of better butter
Will make my batter better.'
So she bought a bit of butter
Better than her bitter butter,
And she put it in her batter,
And it made her batter better,
So 'twas better Betty Botter
Bought a bit of better butter.

('Twas is short for 'It was'.)

Tongue twisters are difficult to say because the same sounds are used, but in words which are only slightly different. So it is easy to get the words and sounds mixed up!

MORE THINGS TO DO

1. Try making up your own tongue twisters.

   ♦ Pick a word.
   ♦ Think of some other words which use the same or very similar sounds.
   ♦ Put them into a sentence which is as awkward to say as possible. Try to give your tongue twisters a rhythm.

2. Try your tongue twisters out on your friends. You could have a tongue-twister-telling competition. Choose a tongue twister. Then see who can say it the fastest, but also clearly and without any mistakes.

13 RIDDLES

Riddles are one of the oldest forms of poetry. They can be found in many different languages and among many peoples. A riddle is a puzzle in words.

See if you can work out the answer to this riddle by reading it carefully and thinking about it.

1
Black I am
And much admired.
Men dig for me
Until they're tired.

The answer is on page 79. Were you right? Was the answer a surprise? Can you see the reasons for the answer? What were the clues in the riddle?

The answers to riddles are not obvious and straightforward, because in a riddle words are used in a tricky way. Riddles remind us that words are slippery things to use and can easily be misleading or misunderstood.

Here is a series of riddles. Many of them rhyme. Try to solve them, on your own, in pairs or small groups. The pictures show the answers. Can you match them up?

2
I'm called by the name of a man
But I'm smaller than a mouse.
When Winter comes I love to be
With my red target near the house.

3
The man that made it didn't need it.
The man that bought it didn't use it.
The man that used it didn't know it.

4
Light as a feather
Nothing in it
A strong man can't hold it
More than a minute.

5
Alive without breath
As cold as death
Never thirsty, ever drinking
All in mail never clinking.

6
Slicked along meddling with rocks
Tore their ears off gradually
Sparkling made them hop and holler
Down a slate-cold throat.

7
This coat can be of many colours
But no-one's worn it yet.
For you can only put it on
When the coat is wet.

8
Some thing I tell
With never a word.
I keep it well
Though it flies like a bird.

9
Long legs, crooked toes
Glassy eyes, snotty nose.

10
Patch upon patch
Without any stitches.
If you tell me this riddle
I'll buy you some breeches.

14 RIDDLES ARE TRANSFORMERS

In a riddle, something ordinary and obvious is turned into something strange and mysterious.

There are many types of riddles. The most common type of riddle is an unusual description which suggests one thing when the answer is something else. Here is an example:

1
Thirty white horses
On a red hill
Now they stamp
Now they champ
Now they stand still.

What does this description suggest to you? What would your answer be? Discuss your answer with a partner.

Now read on for the answer.

In this riddle 'Thirty white horses' stands for teeth. If the white horses are teeth, what is the 'red hill'?

Images

'Thirty white horses' is an image used to describe teeth because teeth are white (or should be) and there are roughly thirty of them – unless you've been eating too many sweets! This type of image is called a *metaphor*. When you use a metaphor, you say that one thing is something else. For example:

The waves of wheat are rippling in the breeze.

We know that wheat isn't really a liquid, but the idea of waves and of rippling can describe the way the wheat moves, so it is a useful metaphor.

Metaphors are not just used in riddles, but in all forms of writing to describe things vividly.

Another way of describing something, instead of saying it *is* something else, is to say it is *like* something else. For example:

The clouds are like wads of cotton wool floating in the sky.

This type of image is called a *simile*. When you use a simile, you say one thing is *like* another thing. 'Cotton wool' is a useful simile for clouds because, like clouds, it is white and fluffy.

Another way of saying something 'is like' something else is to use the word 'as'. 'As green as grass' is a well-known simile; 'as strong as an ox' is another one.

There are four similes in the following riddle. See if you can spot them.

2
    As black as ink and isn't ink
    As white as milk and isn't milk
    As soft as silk and isn't silk
    And hops about like a filly foal. What am I?

What is the answer to this riddle? Here is a clue: The thing described is a bird. Which bird is it? Here is another riddle which uses similes. How many are there, and what is the answer to the riddle?

3
    First I am as white as snow,
    Then as green as grass I grow,
    Next I am as red as blood
    Lastly I'm as black as mud.

More Riddles

Here are some more riddles, this time written by school pupils. See if you can discover the answers. Enjoy yourself, but be careful. Remember that riddles are tricky. The answers might not be that obvious. They might be surprising. If you get stuck on one, then go on to another one and come back to it later. The answers are all shown in the drawings.

4
    I have many sides
    I wear a shiny coat
    And I am friendly with the queen.
    My home is in a pocket,
      a wallet or a purse,
    But I may be found elsewhere.

5
    A thousand feathers on the ground,
    Falling, falling with no sound.
    It dulls one's touch
    And pains the eye
    But brightens the world
    When evening draws nigh.

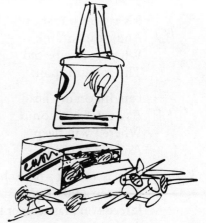

No legs
No wings
No elastic strings.
I'm dropped without care
I fly through the air.

6 I'm hollow
I'm light
But it's all right
For you to hit me
With all your might.
What am I?

7 I come in all shapes and sizes
I'm pulled and pushed about
And scrubbed and washed.
I have hair, but I'm not a head
I have 'paws', but I'm not a dog. What am I?

8 I come in many shapes and sizes
Boxed up and nice.
Open me up and you might find
Something good to eat.
I'm milk or plain
Hollow or filled
The source of a new beginning.

9 Floating through the air
Down with the wind.
In Summer it is green
In Autumn it is red,
Yellow, brown and gold.
In Winter down, down it goes.

10 It's as white as snow
And clears off ink.
When you wipe red
The colour is pink.

11 I am hit on my head
As I enter my home
Where I will sleep
And never roam.

12 This is a thing a household needs
To keep a tidy home.
It feeds on plastic liner bags
And never ever moans.

13
Patiently waiting
Trusting your trap
Of delicate threads
Made from you
Merciless murderer
Lurking
Behind every tree,
Every bush
Snatching whatever you find.

You have now read (and solved!) lots of riddles. You may have noticed that many of them are written as if the subject of the riddle is talking, and describing itself.

MORE THINGS TO DO

Try to write some riddles yourself.

♦ Think of something ordinary to turn into a riddle, such as a beetle.
♦ Note the main details about it.
♦ Compare it with other things either by saying it is like other things (using similes), or it is other things (using metaphors).
♦ Now write your riddle.

How to write a riddle
To show you in more detail how to write a riddle, here is how I wrote my riddle about a beetle.

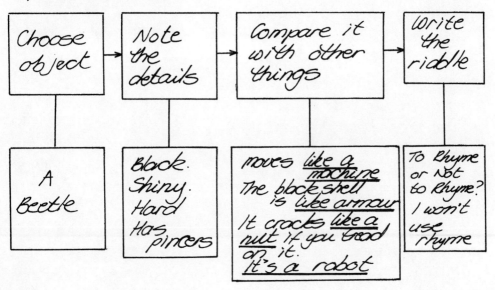

Here is the riddle I wrote:

> An automatic robot
> In shiny black armour
> I creep and crawl everywhere
> Sawing the air
> In a pincer movement.
> I can strike terror into faint hearts
> Yet stepped on
> I crack like a nut.

Now write your own riddle.

REMEMBER
- It's up to you whether or not it rhymes.
- It's a good idea to write the riddle as if the object is talking about itself.
- In a riddle something familiar becomes unusual, something obvious becomes hidden, through the magic of words.

When you've completed a number of them, try your riddles out on a partner, the class, your friends, parents, even your teacher!

15 SHAPE POEMS

You can give poems a sound pattern, using a rhythm and rhyme, or, if you wish, you can make a picture pattern, by turning the words into a picture of what the poem is about. This is called a shape poem. Here is an example.

SNAKE IN THE GRASS   Alison Smith

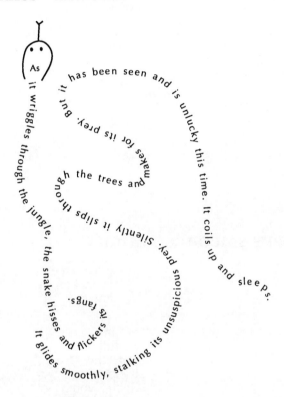

A shape poem can be made with handwriting or with typewriting, using complete sentences. The idea behind it is simple. The words are arranged into the shape of the thing the poem is about. This isn't too difficult, but nevertheless, if you read, as well as look at the following poems carefully, you will see just how much thought and care has gone into them. Choose one or two of them and discuss any interesting points you notice about them in pairs or small groups.

EYESPY   Solera Russell

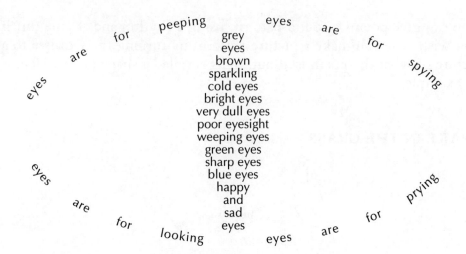

```
                peeping            eyes      are
           for               grey                    for
       are                   eyes
                             brown                       spying
                           sparkling
  eyes                     cold eyes
                           bright eyes
                          very dull eyes
                          poor eyesight
                          weeping eyes
                          green eyes
  eyes                    sharp eyes
                          blue eyes                    prying
        are                happy
             for            and               for
               looking      sad          are
                            eyes    eyes
```

THE HAPPY SAILOR   Rachel Hicks

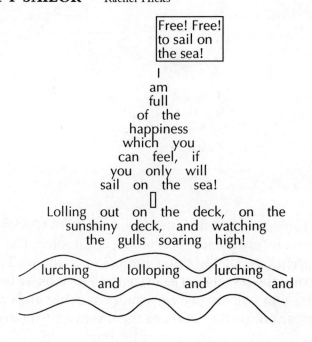

```
                    Free! Free!
                    to sail on
                    the sea!

                        I
                       am
                      full
                     of  the
                    happiness
                   which  you
                  can  feel,  if
                 you  only  will
                sail  on  the  sea!

         Lolling  out  on  the  deck,  on  the
            sunshiny  deck,  and  watching
                the  gulls  soaring  high!

        lurching      lolloping     lurching
                 and            and          and
```

TWO SHAGGY TRAINERS   Rachel Edensor

Unmasted
ships like rowing
boats a-sailing
through the sea.
The rowing boats are
trainers, but they don't seem
that to me. They seem like
two unmasted ships a-sailing
through the sea. They pass
the sea of rug, they pass
the bridge of bed, they
pass the great coal
scuttle or at least
that's what they said.
Two unmasted rowing
boats sailing through
the sea. They might
seem that to you
but they don't seem
that to me. They
seem like two old
shaggy trainers,

And that's all they'll
Ever be.

MORE THINGS TO DO

Make a shape poem of your own.

♦ Think of something with a simple shape that is easy to recognise.
♦ Describe your subject in words.
♦ Draw a faint outline of your subject with a pencil.
♦ Fit your words into the shape. You can do this by arranging your words in lines, or in areas, or both.

You could, if you wish, carefully draw in a few details to make the shape clearer, like in 'The Happy Sailor' on page 52. Or you could just let the words make the picture on their own. If you write (and draw) your shape poems on loose sheets of paper, you can make a wall display with the shape poems created by the whole class.

16 SOUNDS

All spoken words are made from sounds. Normally the sounds a word is made from do not have any obvious connection with its meaning. But there are some words whose sounds imitate actual noises. When the sounds of words imitate actual noises this gives a special sound effect which is called ONOMATOPOEIA (pronounced 'onomatopeeyah'). (The spelling of this word is tricky, so look at it carefully. You will notice that it is not spelt correctly in the poem below.)

Here is a poem by Spike Milligan which is based on this idea and which uses such words. Read it aloud in pairs or small groups.

How many words which imitate actual noises (onomatopoeic words) are there in the poem? Choose three of these words (splash, for example) and say what their sounds suggest to you.

Here are some more examples of writing and poems which use onomatopoeia. Read them aloud in pairs or small groups, and emphasise the onomatopoeic words.

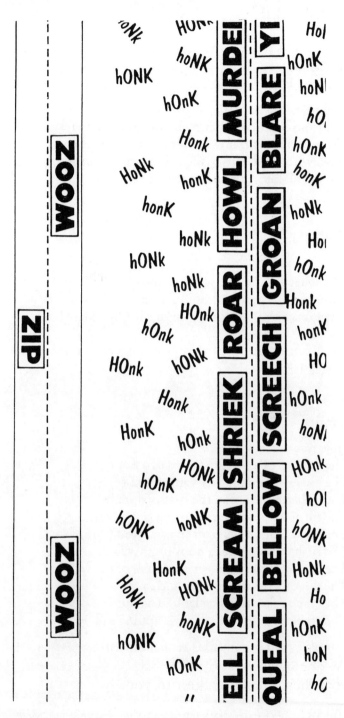

Why did the writer call this poem 'Weekend in the Country'? What point is he making?

J IS FOR JAZZ-MAN   Eleanor Farjeon

Crash and
　　　CLANG!

Bash and
　　　BANG!

And up in the road the Jazz-man sprang!
The One-Man-Jazz-Band playing in the street,
Drums with his Elbows, Cymbals with his Feet,
Pipes with his Mouth, Accordion with his Hand,
Playing all his instruments to Beat the Band!

TOOT and
　　　　Tingle!
HOOT and
　　　　Jingle!

Oh, what a clatter! how the tunes all mingle!
Twenty Children couldn't make as much Noise *as*
The Howling Pandemonium of the One-Man-Jazz!

How does the punctuation of this poem give you some clues as to how
you could read it?

NOISE   Jessie Pope

I like noise.
The whoop of a boy, the thud of a hoof,
The rattle of rain on a galvanised roof.
The hubbub of traffic, the roar of a train,
The throb of machinery numbing the brain,
The switching of wires in an overhead tram,
The rush of the wind, a door on the slam,
The boom of the thunder, the crash of the waves
The din of a river that races and raves,
The crack of a rifle, the clank of a pail,
The strident tattoo of a swift-slapping sail —

From any old sound that the silence destroys
Arises a gamut of soul-stirring joys.
I like noise.

Apart from using onomatopoeic words, how else does the writer
emphasise the sound of the words in this poem?

MORE THINGS TO DO

1. On your own, in pairs or small groups, pick one of the poems above, and practise reading it aloud for a performance to the rest of the class. Concentrate on making your reading bring out the noises very clearly and powerfully.

2. The poem below is a list of new words which the writer has made up to imitate the particular noises he has chosen. Read it aloud.

SOUNDS   Alastair Reid

PLOO is breaking your shoelace.

MRRAAOWL is what cats really say.

TRIS-TRAS is scissors cutting paper.

KINCLUNK is a car going over a manhole cover.

CROOMB is what pigeons murmur to themselves.

PHLOOPH is sitting suddenly on a cushion.

NYO-NYO is speaking with your mouth full.

HARROWOLLOWORRAH is yawning.

PALOOP is the tap dripping in the bath.

RAM TAM GEE PICKAGEE is feeling good.

Are the sounds of these words good imitations of the sounds the writer is trying to imitate?

Now think of some unusual noises yourself and try to make up words whose sounds imitate the noises very closely. For example:

PFFURSST is opening a bottle of fizzy water.

HAAAH-PLIP-PLIP-PLIP-PEEP-EERGH-AGAGAGA-PEEP-PEEP-PEEP is my computer being turned on.

SQUOO is my computer being turned off.

Write down the words you have made up, and give definitions for them. Finally, arrange your onomatopoeic words and their definitions into an order to make a poem.

3. In her poem 'Noise' Jessie Pope gives a list of noises she likes. You could write a list poem of noises you like, or of noises you hate. (See Unit 10 for how to write a list poem)

4. You have produced lists of your own onomatopoeic words for lots of unconnected sounds. Now write a poem about a particular scene in which lots of different noises can be heard at the same time, such as a railway station, a traffic jam, Bonfire Night or a storm. Try to put all the different types of noises in your poem.

5. Onomatopoeic words like those below are often used in comics to give the effect of sound to the pictures. Collect some examples of these words from comics and make a class display of them, by copying them or by cutting them out and making a collage.

AN ANTHOLOGY

An anthology of poems is a collection of poems written by different people. This anthology contains poems for further reading, work and enjoyment. But this collection is only my choice. As time goes on you can choose your own poems and make up your own anthology. You can do this either by writing down the titles of the poems you like (and the titles of the books where you found them) at the back of your exercise book, or in a notebook. Or you can keep a special exercise book in which you copy out poems that you like. Then, in time, you will have your own anthology which you will be able to read and enjoy and which might also tell you something about yourself. So keep your eyes, ears and minds open, because you can find poems anywhere.

HORACE

Much to his Mum and Dad's dismay
Horace ate himself one day.
He didn't stop to say his grace,
He just sat down and ate his face.
"We can't have this!" his Dad declared,
"If that lad's ate, he should be shared."
First his legs and then his thighs,
His arms, his nose, his hair, his eyes . . .
"Stop him someone! Mother cried
"Those eyeballs would be better fried!"
But all too late, for they were gone,
And he had started on his dong . . .
"Oh! foolish child!" the father mourns
"You could have deep-fried that with prawns,
Some parsley and some tartare sauce . . ."
But H. was on his second course:
His liver and his lights and lung,
His ears, his neck, his chin, his tongue;
"To think I raised him from the cot
And now he's going to scoff the lot!"
His Mother cried: "What shall we do?
What's left won't even make a stew . . ."
And as she wept, her son was seen
To eat his head, his heart, his spleen.
And there he lay: a boy no more,
Just a stomach, on the floor . . .
None the less, since it *was* his
They ate it – that's what haggis is.*

* No it isn't. Ed. Haggis is a kind of stuffed black pudding eaten by the Scots and considered by them to be not only a delicacy but fit for human consumption. The minced heart, liver and lungs of a sheep, calf or other animal's organs are mixed with oatmeal, sealed and boiled in maw in the sheep's intestinal stomach-bag and . . .
Excuse me a minute. Ed.

Terry Jones

SOUTHBOUND ON THE FREEWAY

A tourist came in from Orbitville,
parked in the air, and said:

The creatures of this star
are made of metal and glass.

Through the transparent parts
you can see their guts.

Their feet are round and roll
on diagrams – or long

measuring tapes – dark
with white lines.

They have four eyes.
The two in the back are red.

Sometimes you can see a 5–eyed
one, with a red eye turning

on the top of his head.
He must be special –

the others respect him,
and go slow,

when he passes, winding
among them from behind.

They all hiss as they glide,
like inches down the marked

tapes. Those soft shapes,
shadowy inside

The hard bodies – are they
their guts or their brains?

May Swenson

JARGON

Jerusalem, Joppa, Jericho –
These are the cities of long ago.

Jasper, jacinth, jet and jade
of such are jewels for ladies made.

Juniper's green and jasmine's white,
Sweet jonquil is spring's delight.

Joseph, Jeremy, Jennifer, James,
Julian, Juliet – just names.

January, July and June –
Birthday late or birthday soon

Jacket, jersey, jerkin, jeans –
What's the wear for sweet sixteens?

Jaguar, jackal, jumbo, jay –
Came to dinner but couldn't stay.

Jellies, junkets, jumbals, jam –
Mix them up for a sweet-toothed Sam.

To jig, to jaunt, to jostle, to jest –
These are the things that Jack loves best.

Jazz, jamboree, jubilee, joke –
The jolliest words you ever spoke.

From A to Z and Z to A
The joyfullest letter of all is J.

James Reeves

BEFORE THE BIG SCHOOL

Chapped knees
and capped chaps
scarred hands
bruised thighs
cold blasts
rasp fresh
red cheeks
slimy top lips
licking running noses
blue hands
numb feet
Clarks shoes
and big shorts
smells of cabbage
stewed cabbage
butterbeans
and stodgy soggy
plum duff.
Child sweat
grit in cut
scuffed shoes and
Fears
and undone shirts
pink skin
stale smells,
smells of 'Number ones'
on white 'Y' fronts
dry yellow patches
from accidents and drops
and blood on knees
and ankles
Ill-fitting new
sandals
Pigtails and pulling
plaits and buns
undone
ribbons and tugging

Green knickers
and giggles
and navy blue rimmed
specs.
Laughter, tears
'No' and 'Yes MISS'
DINNER ladies
SENT to the Wall
warts and wrinkles
'rebels'
Fights and shouts
'Who wants to play
Armies NO GIRLS'
Touching, cold
and sweating
dustbins, and rubbish
Apple cores,
banana skins
orange peel.
Smiths crisp packets
toilet smells
giggles and touch
toilet paper
tracing paper
sugar and rice paper
Puddles on
plastic chairs
fresh clean baggy shorts
from miserable matrons
Smacks
Red marks
and sticky stars
on white starched collars.
Big grins
and fringes
'Toy Time'
building blocks

and sandpits
grubby fingernails
dirty necks
sand in hair
Hamsters called
'Honey'
rusty bars
sunflower seeds
spliced paper
and dirty corners
Kicking 'K's
Hissing 'S's
Adding and reading
tying ties
and shoe laces
GOLD STARS on card
Storytime
on a plastic mat
plastic patterns
on pink bare legs
gentle voice
and brown-grey hair
kind warm eyes
guinea pig face
furry face
Ringing big bell
and outside gate
mothers and brothers
pushchair, prams
and sweet-shop visits
lolly pop ladies
and green cross code
left and right
smiles and smacks
Scuffed shoes
Chapped knees
capped chaps.

Peter Overton

SNOW AND ICE POEMS

(i)   Our street is dead lazy
espcially in winter.
Some mornings you wake up
and it's still lying there
saying nothing. Huddled
under its white counterpane.

But soon the lorries arrive
like angry mums,
pull back the blankets
and send it shivering
off to work

(ii)   To
boggan?
or not
to boggan?
That is the question.

(iii) Winter
morning.
Snowflakes
for breakfast.
The street
outside
quiet
as a
long
white
bandage.

(iv) The time I like best
is 6 a.m.
and the snow is six inches deep

Which I'm to yet to discover
'cos I'm under the cover
and fast, fast asleep.

Roger McGough

NIGHT MAIL

This is the night mail crossing the border,
Bringing the cheque and the postal order,
Letters for the rich, letters for the poor,
The shop at the corner and the girl next door.
Pulling up Beattock, a steady climb –
The gradient's against her, but she's on time.

Past cotton grass and moorland boulder
Shovelling white steam over her shoulder,
Snorting noisily as she passes
Silent miles of wind-bent grasses.
Birds turn their heads as she approaches,
Stare from the bushes at her black-faced coaches.
Sheep dogs cannot turn her course,
They slumber on with paws across.
In the farm she passes no one wakes,
But a jug in the bedroom gently shakes.

Dawn freshens, the climb is done.
Down towards Glasgow she descends.
Towards the steam tugs yelping down the glade of cranes,
Towards the fields of apparatus, the furnaces
Set on the dark plain like gigantic chessmen.
All Scotland waits for her:
In the dark glens, beside the pale-green lochs,
Men long for news.

Letters of thanks, letters from banks,
Letters of joy from girl and boy,
Receipted bills and invitations
To inspect new stock or visit relations,
And applications for situations
And timid lovers' declarations
And gossip, gossip from all the nations,
News circumstantial, news financial.
Letters with holiday snaps to enlarge in,
Letters from uncles, cousins, and aunts,
Letters to Scotland from the South of France,
Letters of condolence to Highlands and Lowlands,
Notes from overseas to Hebrides –
Written on paper of every hue,
The pink, the violet, the white and the blue,
The chatty, the catty, the boring, adoring,
The cold and official and the heart's outpouring,
Clever, stupid, short and long,
The typed and printed and the spelt all wrong.

Thousands are still asleep
Dreaming of terrifying monsters,
Or a friendly tea beside the band at Cranston's or Crawford's:
Asleep in working Glasgow, asleep in well-set Edinburgh,
Asleep in granite Aberdeen.
They continue their dreams;
But shall wake soon and long for letters,
And none will hear the postman's knock
Without a quickening of the heart,
For who can hear and feel himself forgotten?

W. H. Auden

THE ZEBRA

The zebra is dark and pale.
Snug behind stripes
There are no escapes:
In gaol

Is a habit with him.
He is the doomed
Beast of his mind:
He would rush back in

If you let him out.
His prison warms him. Freedom
Is not what he is about

Or the world . . .
An occasional dream
Now and then . . .
He sleeps curled

And his coat
Warms him – he bears
The print of his bars . . .

It is too late.

John Mole

CONCRETE MIXERS

The drivers are washing the concrete mixers;
Like elephant tenders they hose them down.
Tough grey-skinned monsters standing ponderous,
Elephant-bellied and elephant-nosed,
Standing in muck up to their wheel-caps,
Like rows of elephants, tail to trunk
Their drivers perch on their backs like mahouts,
Sending the sprays of water up.
They rid the trunk-like trough of concrete,
Direct the spray to the bulging sides,
Turn and start the monsters moving.
    Concrete mixers
    Move like elephants
    Bellow like elephants
    Spray like elephants,
Concrete mixers are urban elephants,
Their trunks are raising a city.

Patricia Hubbell

THE DIVER

I put on my aqua-lung and plunge,
Exploring, like a ship with a glass keel,
The secrets of the deep. Along my lazy road
On and on I steal –
Over the waving bushes which at a touch explode
Into shrimps, then closing rock to the tune of the tide;
Over crabs that vanish in a puff of sand.
Look, a string of pearls bubbling at my side
Breaks in my hand –
Those pearls were my breath . . .! Does that hollow hide
Some old Armada wreck in seaweed furled,
Crusted with barnacles, her cannon rusted,
The great *San Philip*? What bullion in her hold?
Pieces of eight, silver crowns, and bars of solid gold?

I shall never know. Too soon the clasping cold
Fastens on flesh and limb
And pulls me to the surface. Shivering, back I swim
To the beach, the noisy crowds, the ordinary world.

Ian Serraillier

urinks the wind
and feeds
on sweat of the leaves

Is little chinks
of mosaic floating
a scatter
of coloured beads

Alighting pokes
with her new black wire
and saffron yokes

On silent hinges
openfolds her wings'
applauding hands
Weaned

from coddling white
to lakedeep air
to blue and green

Is queen

May Swenson

BLACK DOT

a black dot
a jelly tot

a scum-nail
a jiggle-tail

a cool kicker
a sitting slicker

a panting puffer
a fly-snuffer

a high hopper
a belly-flopper

a catalogue
    to make me
        frog.

Libby Houston

THE BULLY ASLEEP

One afternoon, when grassy
Scents through the classroom crept,
Bill Craddock laid his head
Down on his desk, and slept.

The children came round him:
Jimmy, Roger, and Jane;
They lifted his head timidly
And let it sink again.

'Look, he's gone sound asleep, Miss,'
Said Jimmy Adair;
'He stays up all the night, you see;
His mother doesn't care.'

'Stand away from him, children.'
Miss Andrews stooped to see.
'Yes, he's asleep; go on
With your writing, and let him be.'

'Now's a good chance!' whispered Jimmy;
And he snatched Bill's pen and hid it.
'Kick him under the desk, hard;
He won't know who did it.'

'Fill all his pockets with rubbish –
Paper, apple-cores, chalk.'
So they plotted, while Jane
Sat wide-eyed at their talk.

Not caring, not hearing,
Bill Craddock he slept on;
Lips parted, eyes closed –
Their cruelty gone.

'Stick him with pins!' muttered Roger.
'Ink down his neck!' said Jim.
But Jane, tearful and foolish,
Wanted to comfort him.

John Walsh

HERE IS THE NEWS

In Manchester today a man was seen
with hair on top of his head.
Over now straightway to our Northern
    correspondent:
Hugh Snews.

'It's been a really incredible day
here in Manchester. Scenes like this
have been seen here everyday
for years and years. It's now quite certain
no one will be saying anything about this
for months to come. One eyewitness said so.
"Are you sure?" I said.
She said: "No."
Back to you in London.'

All round the world,
newspapers, radio and television
have taken no notice of this story
and already a Prime Minister
has said nothing about it at all.
What next?
Rumour McRumourbungle,
Expert expert in expert experts?

'I doubt it. I doubt whether
anyone *will* doubt it – but I do.'

'What?'

'Doubt it.'

Thank you, Rumour McRumourbungle
But how did it all begin?
As dawn broke in Manchester it soon became clear
It's quite likely there was a lot of air in the air.
An hour after a few minutes had gone,
a couple of seconds passed
and a minute later at 12.15
it was a quarter past twelve.

Suddenly from across the other side of the road,
on the side facing this side,
there was the same road from the other side.
This side was now facing that side
and the road on that other side
was still opposite this.

Then – it happened.
There is no question of this.
In fact – no one has questioned it at all.
Further proof of this comes from the police
who say that a woman held for questioning
was released immediately
because she didn't know the answers
to the questions that no one asked her . . .

So –
it's something of a mystery.
Yes –
it's a mysterious thing to some
and there are some who think
it could
in a mysterious way
be nothing at all.

Michael Rosen

LITTLE FISH

The tiny fish enjoy themselves
in the sea.
Quick little splinters of life,
their little lives are fun to them
in the sea.

SPRAY

It is a wonder foam is so beautiful.
A wave bursts in anger on a rock, broken up
in wild white sibilant spray
and falls back, drawing in its breath with rage,
with frustration how beautiful!

SEA-WEED

Sea-weed sways and sways and swirls
as if swaying were its form of stillness;
and if it flushes against fierce rock
it slips over it as shadows do, without hurting itself.

D.H. Lawrence

RHYME-TIME

I know that poems do not have to rhyme,
And yet I've always liked to hear words chime.
I've noticed, too, that in the world's design
Rhymes play their part, occurring all the time,
Not just in sounds but in the way the fine
Gestures of a tiny plant will mime
In miniature the flourish of a pine,
Proud and lonely on the hill's skyline;
Or how the bright refulgence of moonshine
Is almost echoed in the sheen of lime;
The way the hawthorn foams, a paradigm
For spindrift blossom on the dancing brine.

Oh yes, it's true, all poems do not rhyme
But of the things that I will treasure, nine
Times out of ten, the sounds and objects sign
Themselves on memory and warmly twine
Around the heart and rhythms of the spine
Through using chime and echo.
                      It's no crime –
As verbal savages in grime and slime
Of their poetic darkness whine – to climb
To transcendental heights or try to mime
Deep in the mysteries equally sublime
By rungs or shafts of rhyme. I know that I'm
Old fashioned but I'd never care to sign
A contract that debars the chiming line.
Finally, I ask, what sweeter rhyme
Than your close heartbeat keeping time with mine?

Vernon Scannell

TAKING THE PLUNGE

One day a boy said to a girl in a swimming pool
'I'm going to dive in, are you?' She replied
'No thanks. I bet you can't anyway.' So the boy
got on the diving board and dived and said
'See.' The girl replied 'Flippin 'eck!'
　　(Simon Wilkinson/Margaret Wix Junior School)

Flippin 'eck, cor blimey, strewth,
You're my hero, that's the honest truth.

Lummy, crikey, lordy lord,
It's a long way down from that diving board.

Itchy beard and stone the crows,
Don't you get chlorine up your nose?

Luv a duck and strike me pink,
You're slicker than the soap in the kitchen sink.

Knock me down with a sparrow's feather,
How about us going out together?

Groovy, t'riffic, brill and smashing,
Me 'n' you, we could start things splashing.

Watcha cocky, tara, see ya,
Meet me for a coke in the cafeteria.

Hallelujah and Amen,
If you like this poem you can read it again.

John Mole

THE ARRIVAL

Our train steams slowly in, and we creep to a stop at last.
There's a great unlatching of doors, and the coaches, emptying
    fast,
Let loose their loads of children, and mothers with talkative
    friends,
And sandwiches, flasks, and push-chairs, and apples, and odds
    and ends.

And we move in a crowd together, amid churns and trolleys and
    crates,
Along by a cobbled courtyard, and out through the station gates;
We pass by the waiting taxis; then turn a corner and reach
To where with its flags and cafés the road curves down to the
    beach.

We move in the livelier air, between shining shops and stalls;
Never was such a confusion of coloured bright beach-balls,
And plastic buckets and boats, and ducks of a rubbery blue,
And strings of sandals, and stacks of rock-with-the-name-
    right-through!

Till the many smells which beset us – of onions and cooking
    greens,
Of fumes from the cars and 'buses, of smoke from the noisy inns –
All merge in the one large gust which blows on us broad and
    free,
And catches us, throat and limbs, and heart – the smell of the sea!

John Walsh

MILK FOR THE CAT

When the tea is brought at five o'clock
    And all the neat curtains are drawn with care,
The little black cat with bright green eyes
    Is suddenly purring there.

At first she pretends, having nothing to do,
    She has come in merely to blink by the grate,
But, though tea may be late or the milk may be sour
    She is never late.

And presently her agate eyes
    Take a soft large milky haze,
And her independent casual glance
    Becomes a stiff hard gaze.

Then she stamps her claws or lifts her ears
    Or twists her tail and begins to stir,
Till suddenly all her lithe body becomes
    One breathing trembling purr

The children eat and wriggle and laugh;
    The two old ladies stroke their silk:
But the cat is grown small and thin with desire,
    Transformed to a creeping lust for milk.

The white saucer like some full moon descends
    At last from the clouds of the table above;
She sighs and dreams and thrills and glows,
    Transfigured with love.

She nestles over the shining rim,
    Buries her chin in the creamy sea;
Her tail hangs loose; each drowsy paw
    Is doubled under each bending knee.

A long, dim ecstasy holds her life;
    Her world is an infinite shapeless white,
Till her tongue has curled the last holy drop,
    Then she sinks back into the night.

Draws and dips her body to heap
    Her sleepy nerves in the great arm–chair,
Lies defeated and buried deep
    Three or four hours unconscious there.

Harold Monro

THE FIGHT OF THE YEAR

"And there goes the bell for the third month
and Winter comes out of his corner looking groggy
Spring leads with a left to the head
followed by a sharp right to the body
    daffodils
    primroses
    crocuses
    snowdrops
    lilacs
    violets
    pussywillow
Winter can't take much more punishment
and Spring shows no sign of tiring
    tadpoles
    squirrels
    baalambs
    badgers
    bunny rabbits
    mad march hares
    horses and hounds
Spring is merciless
Winter won't go the whole twelve rounds
    bobtail clouds
    scallywaggy winds
    the sun
    the pavement artist
    in every town
A left to the chin
and Winter's down!
  1 tomatoes
  2 radish
  3 cucumber
  4 onions
  5 beetroot
  6 celery
  7 and any
  8 amount
  9 of lettuce
10 for dinner
Winter's out for the count
Spring is the winner!"

Roger McGough

POETRY JUMP-UP

Tell me if ah seeing right
Take a look down de street

Words dancin
words dancin
till dey sweat
words like fishes
jumpin out a net
words wild and free
joinin de poetry revelry
words back to back
words belly to belly

Come on everybody
come and join de poetry band
dis is poetry carnival
dis is poetry bacchanal
when inspiration call
take yu pen in yu hand
if yu dont have a pen
take yu pencil in yu hand
if yu don't have a pencil
what the hell
so long de feeling start to swell
just shout de poem out

Words jumpin off de page
tell me if Ah seein right
words like birds
jumpin out a cage
take a look down de street
words shakin dey waist
words shakin dey bum
words wit black skin
words wit white skin
words wit brown skin
words wit no skin at all
words huggin up words
an sayin I want to be a poem today
rhyme or no rhyme
I is a poem today
I mean to have a good time

Words feeling hot hot hot
big words feeling hot hot hot
lil words feeling hot hot hot
even sad words cant help
tappin dey toe
to de riddum of de poetry band

Dis is poetry carnival
dis is poetry bacchanal
so come on everybody
join de celebration
all yu need is plenty perspiration
an a little inspiration
plenty perspiration
an a little inspiration

John Agard

Answers to the Riddles

Unit 13
1. Coal
2. A Robin
3. A Coffin
4. Breath
5. A Fish
6. A River
7. Paint
8. A Clock or a Watch
9. A Frog
10. A Cabbage

Unit 14
1. Teeth
2. A Magpie
3. A Bramble
4. A Fifty-Pence Piece
5. Snow
6. A Tennis Ball
7. Skin
8. An Easter Egg
9. A Leaf
10. Tippex
11. A Nail
12. A Dustbin
13. A Spider

Book List

If you would like to read more poems by any of the writers named in this book, then here is a list of authors and titles for you to explore. But remember, no list of writers is ever complete. There are many other books of poems on the shelf, just waiting to be discovered — by you!

I Din Do Nuttin, John Agard, The Bodley Head

Please Mrs Butler, Allen Ahlberg, Kestrel
There is also a joke book which Allen Ahlberg produced with Janet Ahlberg called *The Ha Ha Bonk Book*, Young Puffins

Silver Sand and Snow, Eleanor Farjeon, Michael Joseph Ltd
A selection of Eleanor Farjeon's poems can also be found in *A Puffin Quartet of Poets*, Puffin

Up the Windy Hill, Aileen Fisher, Abelard–Schuman

The Phantom Lollipop Lady Adrian Henri, Methuen

8 a.m. Shadows, Patricia Hubbell, Bolt and Watson

Morning Break and Other Poems, and *The Witch's Brew and Other Poems*, Wes Magee, Cambridge University Press

Nailing the Shadow, Roger McGough, Viking Kestrel

Sky in the Pie, Roger McGough, Puffin

A Book of Milliganimals, and *Silly Verse for Kids,* Spike Milligan, Puffin.

Unspun Socks from a Chicken's Laundry, Spike Milligan, M. and J. Hobbs

Boo to a Goose, John Mole, Peterloo Poets

Custard and Company, Ogden Nash, Kestrel

Magic Mirror and Other Poems, Judith Nicholls, Faber and Faber

Song of the City, and *Salford Road*, Gareth Owen, Fontana Young Lions

Collected Poems for Children, James Reeves, Heinemann

Collected Poems, Theodore Roethke, Faber and Faber

Wouldn't you like to know?, Michael Rosen, Puffin

When did you last wash your feet?, Michael Rosen, Fontana Young Lions

Mastering the Craft, Vernon Scannell, Pergamon

New and Collected Poems, Vernon Scannell, Robson Books

Happily Ever After, Ian Serraillier, Oxford University Press
A selection of Ian Serraillier's poems can also be found in *A Puffin Quartet of Poets*

To Mix with Time, May Swenson, Charles Scribner

Two anthologies which you might enjoy reading are:

The Hippo Book of Funny Verse
Mary had a Crocodile and Other Funny Animal Verse, poems selected by Jennifer Curry, Puffin